Original title:
Purpose and Puns: A Life's Guide

Copyright © 2025 Creative Arts Management OÜ
All rights reserved.

Author: Nathaniel Blackwood
ISBN HARDBACK: 978-1-80566-106-1
ISBN PAPERBACK: 978-1-80566-401-7

Scripting Smiles in the Story of Life

In a world of rhymes and playful jest,
We dance through days, always at our best.
With laughter as our map and joy our guide,
Each chuckle serves as an amusing ride.

When troubles knock, we answer with a grin,
A wink at fate, let the fun begin!
For every fumble, let's turn them around,
Finding the punchline is where joy is found.

With puns as our pluck, we leap and bound,
In silly tales, our spirits are unbound.
We sprinkle humor, a dash of delight,
Crafting our moments, oh what a sight!

So let's script our smiles, embracing the game,
In this wild adventure, we're never the same.
With laughter as treasure, our hearts will ignite,
In the story of life, let's bask in the light!

The Punny Path to Clarity

When life feels like a tangled kite,
Just give it a giggle, and hold it tight.
A jest in the wind, and you'll soon find,
That laughter can clear the fog from the mind.

With every pun that you toss to the air,
You lighten the load, shedding every care.
So step on the path that's paved with delight,
And let chuckles guide you into the night.

Fables of Fulfillment and Fun

Listen closely, my friend, to this tale,
Of a wise old cat who learned how to sail.
He caught fish with jokes, not with a hook,
And wrote his own fables in a dusty book.

He roamed through the valleys with chuckling hearts,
Finding joy in the quirks, mastering arts.
With each twist of fate, a grin would arise,
As laughter rolled in like waves 'neath the skies.

Quips for the Questing Heart

On the road to a dream, don't forget to laugh,
Life's better served with a side of the daft.
A quip in your pocket, so light on your feet,
Sparks joy like a flame, making the journey sweet.

When troubles loom large, try a clever twist,
It's humor's embrace that you simply can't miss.
For every odd turn leads to something bright,
With laughter as lantern, you'll find your way right.

The Art of Living Lightly

In a world that seems heavy, why not be light?
Pack up all your worries, let them take flight.
A wink and a nod, with humor to spare,
Elevates your heart and puts joy in the air.

Embrace all the quirks, let your laughter ring,
For life is a canvas; make it a swing.
Brush strokes of fun painted vivid and bold,
Create a bright story, let the magic unfold.

Finding Joy in the Jests

Life's a game of cheerful tricks,
Where laughter's just the best of picks.
A wink, a smile, a playful poke,
In every jest, there's joy bespoke.

When troubles come, just crack a grin,
Turn frowns to laughs, let joy begin.
A silly dance or goofy face,
In every jest, we find our place.

So grab a pun, or two or three,
And let the giggles set you free.
For life is bright when shared in play,
With every laugh, we find our way.

In jests, we find our hearts' delight,
A playful spirit makes it bright.
So take a chance, don't stay aloof,
For laughter's here, just be the goof!

Lighthearted Lessons on the Road

In every bend, a twist awaits,
With humor riding on our fates.
A pun or two can lighten loads,
On this odd journey down the roads.

When traffic jams bring on the frowns,
Just sing a song, wear silly crowns.
For life's a ride, and what a show,
With laughter as our way to go.

Share a joke or try a pun,
In tedium, make the mundane fun.
With every mile, our spirits lift,
The best of gifts is joy, no thrift.

So map your course with funny signs,
And let your heart draw funky lines.
For lightness makes the journey sweet,
As laughter dances on our feet!

The Comedy of Intentions

We strive and laugh in awkward ways,
Each stumble churns a funny phase.
With every goal that starts to drift,
We find that humor is the gift.

When plans go wrong and hiccups start,
Just throw a pun with all your heart.
A wink, a nudge, an elbow nudge,
We'll laugh it off; we'll never judge.

For every dream we pursue with glee,
There's a twist that sets us free.
In life's own sketch, we find the punch,
At every twist, we learn to crunch.

So chase your dreams, they're meant to dance,
In muddled paths, just take a chance.
With laughter leading, never fear,
The comedy of life is here!

Whimsical Wanderings and Wonder

In lands of whimsy, dreams take flight,
Where fun and folly twirl with light.
Each step we take, a wonder grows,
In laughter's glow, the spirit glows.

A jester's heart can show the way,
Through every twist, we'll laugh and play.
For in absurdity, we find delight,
In silly antics taking flight.

With every road, a new surprise,
A funky dance beneath the skies.
So wander free, embrace the quirk,
For whimsy sows the joy that works.

In whispers soft, life's lessons sing,
The happiest tune that joy can bring.
So bow to humor, play along,
In whimsical tales, we all belong!

Serendipity's Satire

A squirrel with a plan, no acorn in sight,
Stashes nuts in a tree, thinks he'll be all right.
He laughs at his fortune, all leafy and fleeced,
But winter's just waiting, all sharp and unleased.

With each silly blunder, a tumble through life,
He juggles his dreams, amidst laughter and strife.
In the end, he finds joy in the silly absurd,
Even when he mistakes a twig for a bird.

Beyond the Punchline

A jester in the corner, with pie on his face,
Makes light of the troubles, a true comic grace.
He winks at the audience, the laughter erupts,
While balancing life's whims like a clown that disrupts.

With every wisecrack, the truth takes a twist,
Every sorrow in life just a punchline missed.
He spins tales of glory, the mundane to grand,
Making punchlines from moments that were never quite planned.

A Journey of Jest

A traveler wanders with jokes on his lips,
Finding laughter like treasure on his comedic trips.
He stumbles on wisdom wrapped in a jest,
Collecting the giggles, he's never distressed.

Each step tells a story, a jest to unfold,
With puns that sparkle, like jewels made of gold.
He shares what he finds, the laughter, the fun,
All while chasing shadows from the morning sun.

The Comedic Compass

In a world filled with chaos, he follows the joke,
A compass of laughter, where logic's bespoke.
He roams through the riddles, the quirks of the day,
Finding the humor in life's crazy array.

Like a map made of giggles, he charts out the path,
With every wrong turn, he embraces the math.
Each punchline a marker, guiding him through,
Turning life's serious into a sprightly view.

Crafting Cheerful Chronicles

In a circus of dreams, we clown around,
Juggling wishes, where joy is found.
Each laugh's a page, we scribble and trace,
With silly grins, we embrace the chase.

We dance on the edge of silly delight,
Tickling fancies, hearts take flight.
With jest and giggles, we write our tale,
Sailing on laughter, we set our sail.

In each blooper, wisdom does hide,
Wit wraps around us like a warm tide.
A slip, a bobble, it's all in fun,
We're the stars in our comic run.

So toast to the giggles, the gaffes we make,
A life full of joy is the best kind of cake.
With warmth and laughter, as our guide,
Every misstep a new joyride.

The Silly Side of Self-Discovery

Who says finding self needs a serious face?
Let's wear our charm like a silly lace.
In quirky hats, we'll strut with flair,
Discovering truths in everywhere.

Flip-flops on feet, mismatched in style,
We'll figure it out, but all with a smile.
Wit is our mirror, reflecting the fun,
In a world full of jest, we all are one.

Dance like a chicken, sing out of tune,
Life's a wild ride, and it's none too soon.
In verses of laughter, our spirits entwine,
In this carnival of quirks, everything's fine.

So leap into nonsense, let your heart play,
With giggles and quirks, we'll brighten the day.
Through this silliness, we'll surely see,
The braver we are, the more we can be.

Echoes of Laughter in Life's Labyrinth

In the maze of life, we trip and we crawl,
With a wink and a smile, we'll conquer it all.
Around each corner, a chuckle lies,
Navigating joy with gleaming eyes.

With riddles and rhymes, the path becomes clear,
Each giggle a guide, we have nothing to fear.
So follow the echoes, let laughter align,
For every twist leads to a punchline.

Lost in the comedy of all life's plans,
We'll dance through the puzzles with our happy hands.
With whimsy our map, we'll find our way,
In the tapestry of laughter, we choose to stay.

So here's to the laughs that lighten our load,
In this maze of life, let joy explode.
With every turn, let our spirits be free,
In the echo of laughter, we'll always be.

Jests for the Journey Ahead

As we embark on life's whimsical quest,
With jokes packed tight, we're surely blessed.
A sprinkle of humor in every stride,
Laughter our lantern, joy our guide.

With each little quip, our burdens take flight,
Turning troubles to giggles, oh what a sight!
In the story we craft, let amusement be lead,
For jokes are the compass, guiding our tread.

So bring on the gaffes, the blunders, the bliss,
In the comic embrace, we find our sweet kiss.
Let's laugh while we wander this curious lace,
For the heart beats stronger with each funny place.

So gather your funnies, let's take a chance,
Life's a grand party; let's lead the dance!
With humor our ally, we'll paint the road bright,
With jests for the journey, let's soar like a kite.

The Tale of Intentional Chuckles

In a land where laughter bursts,
Every jest quenches the thirst.
A pun here, a joke over there,
Life's a circus, if you dare.

With each step, the giggles flow,
Juggling dreams, putting on a show.
A wink, a twist, a frolicsome tease,
Life's best punchlines, if you please.

So gather 'round, don't hold back,
The road ahead's a merry track.
With wit in hand, we'll take a chance,
In this dance, we all enhance.

So laugh at life, what's the harm?
With a quip or two, we'll stay warm.
As smiles bloom, we'll know it's true,
The jest of living starts with you.

Navigating Joy's Waters

In a boat made of wishes, we float,
Rowing with laughter, what a note!
Oars made of giggles, sails made of cheer,
Charting our course, we know no fear.

The currents of joy push us along,
Riding the waves, we sing our song.
Navigating life with a chuckle or two,
Splashing in puddles, just me and you.

A treasure chest full of puns and delight,
Sparkling with wisdom, our compass is bright.
In every ripple, we find a smile,
Sailing through storms, it's all worth the while.

With every wave, we dance and glide,
Joy's waters carry us, side by side.
Together we conquer the sea of good times,
In the rhythm of laughter, our spirit climbs.

A Quip for Every Quest

With laughter as armor, we take our stand,
In quests of whimsy, we're hand in hand.
Every challenge a punchline, so clever and neat,
In the journey of jest, there's no defeat.

To the mountains of giggles, we dare to climb,
With jokes as our guides, we conquer time.
From valleys of fun, we'll never stray,
On this path of humor, we find our way.

When life throws curveballs, we'll catch them with glee,
Turning frowns into grins, you'll see.
With a quip for a potion, we'll take a sip,
On this merry adventure, let's never trip.

So onward we march, toward laughter's embrace,
In every corner, we find our place.
With joy as our compass, we'll surely succeed,
In quests full of chuckles, it's laughter we need.

The Riddle of Reverie

In dreams we wander, with laughter to chase,
A riddle unravels, at a merry pace.
What's fuzzy and funny, with tickles inside?
A life filled with giggles, where joy cannot hide.

Each puzzle a chuckle, each think a delight,
In the shadows of whimsy, we dance in the light.
What's soft and absurd, and floats like a breeze?
Silly questions and quirks that bring us to our knees.

When serious knocks, we'll answer with cheer,
With witty comebacks, we'll loosen the fear.
What's heavy as laughter, yet light as a sigh?
It's the riddles we cherish that help us get by.

So gather your thoughts, let's ponder a while,
For in every riddle, you'll find a big smile.
In the heart of the puzzle, there lies a refrain,
A whimsical world, where we dance in the rain.

A Twist of Fate and Fun

Life's a dance, feet may slip,
With each misstep, laughter's grip.
Chasing dreams like a runaway cat,
Sometimes you land in a silly hat.

A fortune cookie once told me so,
Stick to your path, but don't move slow.
Jokes and giggles light the way,
So tickle your fate, come what may.

Plans may crumble like flaky crust,
In chaos, find the humor you trust.
When life gives you lemons, make a pie,
Just don't forget to laugh as you try.

In a world of twists, embrace the spin,
With laughter's help, you'll always win.
As fate unfolds, just seize the run,
For every hiccup, there's always fun.

Sunny Satires

Woke up to sunshine and a grin,
Decided today to dive right in.
But socks on hands? A fashion faux pas,
Laughter spilled out like a soda straw.

Banana peels on a slickened floor,
Slide right in like a joke encore.
But laughter's light can cure all woes,
Turning stumbles into comedy shows.

When the sun's up, let giggles unfold,
A pocketful of joy, more precious than gold.
Because what's more bright than a well-timed joke?
Even life's tough can't break the folks who poke.

So roam with glee, don't let it rest,
For humor's a sail, let it be your quest.
As shadows loom and troubles creep,
Bring out the chuckles, dig down deep.

The Grin that Guides

In the mirror, a funny face,
With every grin, find your place.
A wink adds magic to a mundane day,
And silly dances lead the way.

Life's a puzzle, some pieces in jest,
Find the laughs, we've all been blessed.
When fate's a riddle, laugh it out loud,
Each giggle's a gift, wear it proud.

Each tumble down the bumpy lane,
Becomes a jest, not just a pain.
Drop the frown, just twist and twirl,
With a grin like this, you'll rock the world.

So when the clouds start to appear,
Tickle your worries, with joy persevere.
For every riddle that life may throw,
A chuckle at least is the way to go.

Joyful Jests on the Journey

Set forth on paths both tricky and tight,
With jest in hand, make it bright.
A tickle of joy in every step,
In laughter, dear friend, we're all adept.

The road may twist and take a U-turn,
But smile through lessons we all learn.
For every bump and each curvy slice,
Sprinkle some humor, oh how nice!

Rain clouds may gather, but don't you fret,
Find a silver lining where you bet.
With every chuckle, the world seems fine,
As you dance through the rain, sip that wine.

From sunny trails to shadows passed,
Find gold in laughter that always lasts.
So here we roll, with joy we glide,
For the journey's fun, our hearts collide.

Laugh Lines of Life

In the garden of giggles, flowers bloom bright,
With humor as sunshine, dispelling the night.
We dance through the chaos, a whimsical spree,
Turning stumbles to chuckles, just you wait and see.

Life's riddles and jokes, like a jigsaw we weave,
Each piece adds a laugh, more than you can believe.
When plans go awry, wear a smile, don't pout,
For laughter's the remedy, there's no doubt.

A pun a day keeps the blues far away,
Like a clown in a circus, we twirl and we sway.
With friends by our side, there's no room for gloom,
As we paint the world's canvas in mirth's vibrant plume.

From silly mishaps, great tales are composed,
We'll treasure these moments, with joy unopposed.
So raise up a glass, to the light-hearted cheer,
In the book of our lives, let laughter steer clear.

The Chortle Chronicles

In a world full of quirks, we write our own script,
With humor as ink, let the laughter be zipped.
The mischief of life, we sketch with a grin,
Transforming the frowns into joy from within.

A tickle of wit, and we're off on a quest,
Searching for punchlines, never needing a rest.
With snickers and snorts, confusion unravels,
In the library of giggles, each funny scene travels.

If trouble comes knocking, we'll slip on a shoe,
That squeaks with each step, as we laugh at the view.
For the stars are just giggles that light up the night,
Our journey is paved with chuckles in flight.

So gather your friends, let's conquer the jest,
With humor our armor, we'll strive for the best.
In the chronicles written, it's laughter we pen,
And the tales that we tell, they'll echo again.

Navigating with Nonsense

A compass of chuckles to guide us along,
In the map of our days, where all can belong.
Each bump in the road brings a laugh on the way,
As we seek out the silly, come what may.

From ducks in high hats to kangaroos in shoes,
Reality bends, as we choose to amuse.
With nonsense our beacon, we'll sway to the tune,
Of whimsy's fine rhythm beneath the bright moon.

When life gives us lemons, we'll make lemonade,
With a twist of the tongue, puns serenely played.
Like squirrels in a dance, we'll leap and we'll bound,
In a playground of giggles, joy's always around.

So grab your own quirk, let's set sail with glee,
On the ship of absurdity, wild and free.
With laughter as currency, how rich we shall be,
Navigating this nonsense, eternally carefree.

The Lightness in Life's Load

With a wink and a chuckle, we lighten the weigh,
Finding glee in the moments that often decay.
Like bubbles in soda, we rise and we pop,
Turning burdens to breezes, we'll never just stop.

In the circus of living, we juggle our dreams,
With laughter as safety, we mend all the seams.
A pratfall can spark joy, just slip and then grin,
For each tumble we take, brings a dance underneath skin.

So let the world twirl; we'll sway in its spree,
With jokes as our cushions, so soft and so free.
When worries intrude, we'll tickle the claws,
Turning frowns into joy, with a wink and applause.

For in this grand theater, we play our own role,
With whimsy our script, we embrace the whole.
Join hands in this jest, where lightness is found,
In the laughter we share, our hearts will resound.

The Jocular Journey

In a world of laughs and cheer,
The road is bright, the end is near.
With every chuckle, wisdom grows,
Beneath the skin, humor glows.

Take a step, don't slip and fall,
Life's a joke at the carnival.
Giggles chase away the frowns,
Laughter spins the ups and downs.

Tales of Cosmic Comedy

Stars chuckle in the vast above,
Planets spin with a burst of love.
Galaxies play in their dance so wild,
Even black holes can be beguiled.

A comet's tail can tickle your mind,
As jokes are cosmic, well-defined.
Space-time giggles, what a view,
Join the fun, come laugh anew.

Directions from Delight

Follow the signs, they're full of glee,
To find the humor, just let it be.
A twist in the road may make you grin,
Seek the laughter, let it begin.

Detours lead to smiles along the way,
With every pun, you seize the day.
Life's a map with laughter marked,
In joy's embrace, we're all embarked.

The Funny Roadmap

On this roadmap, find your jest,
Every mile leads to a fest.
Pit stops for puns, take a break,
Fill your tank with joy, for goodness' sake!

Winding paths of quirky sights,
Giggles echo through the nights.
With each twist and every turn,
Discover lessons, joyful and stern.

The Light Footprint of Laughter

In every step, a giggle blooms,
Like flowers sprouting in our rooms.
Chase the joy, don't take a chance,
Life's a dance, a silly dance.

With every joke, a shadow fades,
Where troubles linger, laughter wades.
Tickle your thoughts, let spirits sail,
In the whimsy, we shall prevail.

Turn frowns upside down in delight,
Life's a circus, come take a bite.
The light footprint of joy we tread,
With a gentle nudge and grin widespread.

So laugh aloud, let spirits take flight,
In this journey, we rewrite the night.
Each chuckle echoed, a vibrant art,
In the gallery of every heart.

Kidding Around with Existence

Life's a game of jesters and jest,
Where every challenge is a fun test.
Wear a smile like a bouncy hat,
And laugh loud at the silliest spat.

Frogs in suits make quite the show,
While toasters dance with a merry glow.
In numbers, we find the quirkiest sums,
A world where giggles and joy becomes.

Each quip's a ticket to the jest,
To ride the waves and feel the zest.
From tiny puns to jokes that soar,
In the lightness, we find much more.

So roll with humor, let spirits twirl,
In this cosmic dance, watch laughter unfurl.
Kidding around, we find our way,
In every jest, a brighter day.

The Comedic Cartographer

With a map in hand, I chart the scene,
Where smiles sprout, and laughter's keen.
Each silly stride across the page,
Leads us deeper in joyous stage.

Crossing the bridges of quirky tales,
Where humor stirs, and mischief prevails.
In every corner, a chuckle found,
A treasure of mirth that knows no bound.

The landmarks marked with puns and glee,
Guide us through life's quirky spree.
Navigate with joy as your guide,
In this comic world, let laughter abide.

So grab your compass, let humor inspire,
With each laugh, we climb ever higher.
In laughter's realm, we find our map,
The comedic cartographer breaks the trap.

Dreams in Drollery

In the land of dreams, the jokes take flight,
Where giggles echo through the night.
Imagination spins a comical tale,
With laughter's breeze filling every sail.

Witty whispers on the moonlit stream,
Puns float by like a laugh's sweet dream.
Chasing shadows of the smiley sun,
In the drollery, we find the fun.

With each night's rest, new humor springs,
A symphony of joy that softly sings.
Tickle the mind in slumber's embrace,
In dreams, we play a whimsical chase.

So drift away on laughter's wings,
Where the heart of joy forever clings.
In every dream, let the fun unfurl,
In drollery's grip, we dance and twirl.

Revelations in Riddles

What has a head, but cannot think?
A pen, my friend, that's quite the link.
We scribble dreams and jokes in line,
Unraveling smiles, oh so divine.

Every twist and turn is wisdom's game,
Life sends riddles, never dull and tame.
So laugh at the questions, don't take it hard,
For answers are treasures left in the yard.

From ticklish thoughts to silly schemes,
Each riddle we solve feeds our wild dreams.
With every quip that we unveil,
The laughter's the wind that fills our sail.

So ponder away, let confusion creep,
The joy in the journey makes our hearts leap.
Embrace the quirky, the unexpected fun,
For life is a puzzle, and we've just begun.

Giggles Along the Path

Stumbling forward, tripping in glee,
Who knew that life was a comedy spree?
With every misstep, a chuckle is born,
In moments of folly, we feel less worn.

The road is a stage, and we play our part,
With laughter to weave into the heart.
A slip on a banana, a joke gone awry,
We find the fun in the reason why.

In the garden of giggles, we plant our seed,
Water it gently, just what we need.
A smile's a flower, watch it bloom bright,
Colorful petals dance in delight.

So skip through the day, with a wink and a smile,
Let humor be with you, mile after mile.
For life's little quirks, celebrate and sway,
In the rhythm of laughter, let's play all day.

The Shtick and the Soul

In the theater of life, we take our seats,
With buckets of laughter and popcorn treats.
Watch as the antics unfold with flair,
For joy's the main act, and love's in the air.

With every punchline, we find our way,
Life takes on a rhythm, a playful ballet.
The humor we share, a bond so sweet,
Connecting us all, a delightful feat.

Life's a screenplay, with twists and turns,
Each laugh a lesson, our passion burns.
From pratfalls to quips, we share our role,
Embrace the silliness deep in the soul.

So gather your friends for this joyous ride,
Life's the best comedy; let laughter abide.
With a wink and a giggle, we dance through the day,
In the shtick of our souls, we find our way.

Chronicles of Cheerful Choices

Every morning, we wake with a grin,
What merry mischief will today begin?
Socks that don't match, or a hat on the dog?
The joy of the choice escapes every fog.

Flip a coin, let it guide your feet,
With serendipity, life's a fun beat.
From ice cream for breakfast to dancing in rain,
Each cheerful choice is a win, not a pain.

Beneath clouds of laughter, rainbows appear,
In the chronicles told, we have nothing to fear.
Choose to be silly, let worries abate,
In the book of life's humor, oh what a fate!

So grab your notebook, let's write today,
With every choice, let the chuckles play.
For in each decision, big or small,
Lies the sweet taste of joy, let's savor it all.

Chuckles at the Crossroads

In the midst of choices, a jester stands tall,
With arrows of laughter directed at all.
Do I take the left path or wander to the right?
Either way, I'll chuckle into the night.

Bumping into fate with a pie in my face,
Every misstep feels like a comical chase.
The compass is broken, but it's okay,
For giggles and jokes lead me on my way.

So here at the junction, I twirl and I sway,
In this carnival life, there's always a play.
With each silly slip, I find joy in the fall,
Laughter's the currency, it's worth more than all.

So if you feel lost, don't wear a frown wide,
Join me in laughter, on this whimsical ride.
For paths twist and turn, but it's all in good fun,
A life full of chuckles can't ever be done.

Mirthful Motives

With each morning's light, I craft a new scheme,
To sprinkle some giggles and dance like a dream.
Motives are masked in a jumble of cheer,
With slapstick and joy, there's nothing to fear.

I'll juggle my worries, all tossed in the air,
They bounce off the walls, oh, life is so rare!
Why take things too seriously, tell me, my friend?
When laughter can lead us, around every bend.

So put on a grin, let's waltz through the fray,
With quirky perspectives, we'll brighten the day.
Every motive we have, has a spark of delight,
In this funny dance, we'll twirl through the night.

Our mirthful intentions can lift up the gloom,
Like daisies in sunlight, we'll always bloom.
Chasing the silliness, let's make a pact,
To find joy in madness, and never look back.

Whimsy in the Wilderness

In the woods of the wild, where the trees laugh aloud,
   I waltz with the squirrels, oh, ain't I so proud!
Every rustle of leaves is a chuckle in disguise,
   Nature's a comedian, oh, how it complies!

   I slip on a pebble, roll down a hill,
The critters all cheer, it's quite the thrill!
With a hop and a skip, I dance with the breeze,
   In this playful sanctuary, I do just as I please.

The sunbeams are giggling, the shadows play peek,
   While I join the chorus with a jig and a squeak.
Every branch is a stage, every rock is a prop,
   In this whimsical wild, I'll never stop.

So let's wander this path with the joy of a child,
   For life's filled with magic, all goofy and wild.
In this fairy-tale woods, where laughter is free,
We'll find whimsy together, just you wait and see.

A Spectrum of Smiles

A rainbow of giggles appears in the sky,
Every color a chuckle, you'll see them fly by.
From red to bright yellow, the hues dance around,
In the spectrum of smiles, pure happiness found.

With blues like a laugh and greens full of glee,
Each moment we savor is wild and carefree.
Puns that slice through like a knife made of fun,
We gather together 'til the laughter is done.

Oranges and pinks blend, weaving tales in the air,
With jokes that we share, there's joy everywhere.
In this canvas of life, where humor's the art,
Every smile we paint, is a piece of the heart.

So wear your bright grin, let it shine in the sun,
For laughter's contagious, and oh, what a run!
In this vibrant adventure, let joy intertwine,
With a spectrum of smiles, we'll always be fine.

Luminous Laughter

When life hands you lemons, make a stand,
Squeeze the zest, let humor expand.
A joke in your pocket, a grin on your face,
The world is a stage, a comedic place.

With every mishap, let giggles ensue,
Like slipping on marbles, find joy that is true.
Embrace every blunder, dance with the fright,
For laughter's the beacon that shines through the night.

A jester in life brings brightness to gloom,
With puns as our fuel, we'll make chaos bloom.
In the garden of jest, let joy find its root,
Life's a silly dance, so shake off your suit.

So let's toast to the whims and the wit we can share,
In the tapestry woven, there's laughter to spare.
With friends that are funny, and smiles that ignite,
Each chuckle a spark, spreading warmth and delight.

The Quest for Quirkiness

In a world of straight lines, find curves that enthrall,
Let oddness be cherished, embrace what seems small.
A hat worn askew, mismatched socks on parade,
In the festival of quirks, let no fun be delayed.

Seek laughter in tales that twist and expand,
Where rabbits wear sunglasses, and donuts wear bands.
Chase dreams on a unicycle, ride through the park,
In laughter's embrace, we'll ignite our own spark.

A peculiar jingle, an unusual rhyme,
Makes every odd moment worth savoring time.
So gather the curious, the strange, and the mad,
With riddles and riddles, we'll feast and be glad.

Join the quirky brigade, there's magic to find,
In jest and in whimsy, our laughter aligned.
Let's dance with the odd, like ducks in a line,
In the quest for the quirky, we dare to shine.

The Fable of Frolic

Once in a field where the daisies play,
A fox wore a bow tie, brightening the day.
He'd tell clever tales of his mischief and schemes,
While tickling the fowl who drifted in dreams.

With squirrels as jesters and owls as the crowd,
They'd laugh at the antics, both silly and loud.
A hiccuping hare tried to hop through a dance,
Each blunder a giggle, a whimsical chance.

When night would fall softly, the stars took to cheer,
They'd wink with a twinkle, inviting us near.
So frolic and frolic, with jesters in sight,
A fable of laughter, in peace and delight.

Let stories of joy fill the corners of night,
In every small chuckle, our hearts feel so light.
A fable forever of frolic and fun,
In the garden of laughter, our souls become one.

Anecdotal Anchors

With anchors made of stories, we float on the sea,
Each tale a buoy, keeping spirits so free.
A fish that speaks French and sings on its way,
Makes waves of adventure, come join in the play.

In harbors of humor, we gather with glee,
With skits on the shore, as bright as can be.
A lighthouse of laughter guides sailors at night,
As giggles our compass, we sail towards delight.

We tether our hearts to the anchors we hold,
Each chuckle a treasure, more precious than gold.
Through storms and through squalls, we won't drift apart,
Anecdotes like life-rafts, float dreams from the heart.

So let the waves crash, let the winds blow us wide,
With laughter as our captain, we'll sail with pride.
In the ocean of jest, let our spirits be grand,
As anecdotal anchors, we're never in bland.

Humorous Hues in Life's Canvas

In shades of laughter, we paint our days,
With silly brushes in whimsical ways.
Every slip, every trip adds flair to the scene,
Where giggles abound, life's a fun machine.

Colorful moments, like rainbows in flight,
We find in the absurd, our purest delight.
So spill that paint, let the colors collide,
In this merry mess, let your joy be your guide.

Life's palette rich, with quirks and with quips,
Paint us a smile, let humors eclipse.
From bloopers to blunders, all chalked up as wins,
In this canvas of laughter, true living begins.

Chasing Chuckles and Clarity

In the chase for a giggle, clarity's found,
Like tripping on laughter, it's joy that's unbound.
Embrace every tickle, every joke that you hear,
For wisdom hides well within the sincere.

Through tangled tales, our sanity grows,
In silly mishaps, life cleverly flows.
Chasing those chuckles, we stumble on fate,
In laughter we trust, never too late!

When riddles unfold, and we laugh at the tale,
Our minds fill with clarity, resilience prevails.
With each little jest, we lighten the load,
On this road trip called life, let humor be our code.

The Riddles of Existence

What's the point of a pun if laughter's the prize?
As riddles entwined, they twist and arise.
With every odd question, a smile's the reply,
In this game of life, we just aim to fly.

Finding the reason in a playful jest,
Turns every soft chuckle into life's very best.
For who needs a map when the road's full of fun?
Just laugh with the answers beneath the sun.

The riddle's the journey, not just the end,
The punchline's a lift, on joy we depend.
In the quip of the night, under stars shiny bright,
We unravel existence, laughter ignites.

Wit's Roadmap to Riches

In the riches of laughter, we find treasure's gold,
With wit as our compass, adventure unfolds.
Each quip a direction, each pun a signpost,
On this road paved with humor, it's joy that we boast.

Mapping out giggles through valleys of glee,
Navigate life with a chuckle, carefree.
When challenges arise, don't pout, just grin,
In the spirit of laughter, we always win.

A map drawn in jest, with playful grooves,
Leads us to moments that joyfully prove.
That riches aren't measured in wealth or in things,
But in laughter and love that each wise heart brings.

Delights and Directions

In a world where laughter flows,
A map made of giggles shows.
Each turn a joke, a playful jest,
Adventure awaits, come be our guest.

With every stumble, find a grin,
Life's a dance, so let's begin.
Step to the left, trip to the right,
Falling down, but what a sight!

On roads paved with silly schemes,
Chase your wildest, wackiest dreams.
A pot of gold at the end of fun,
Where every laugh has just begun.

So don your cape, embrace the mirth,
In this land of playful worth.
For each step you take, make it shine,
With laughter, life feels just divine.

The Art of Lighthearted Living

With smiles as brushes and joy as paint,
Crafting moments that feel quite quaint.
Each stroke a giggle, a whimsical cheer,
Life's masterpiece, painted dear.

Dancing through the everyday grind,
A sprinkle of humor is what we find.
When life hands lemons, squeeze them tight,
Turn them to lemonade, make it light!

Chasing rainbows on a sunny day,
In puddles of laughter, we love to play.
So grab your palette, don't be shy,
Create a canvas where spirits fly.

With every misstep, find a new hue,
Brush strokes of fun, until we're through.
Art is alive, and we're the muse,
In lighthearted living, feel the fuse.

Winks and Wisdom

A wink of mischief, a quick little nudge,
In the game of life, we're the ones to judge.
With riddles in pockets and puns on the go,
We twinkle and giggle, putting on a show.

In moments of chaos, let's crack a smile,
Turn worries to laughter, it's totally worthwhile.
For wisdom is often a whimsical twist,
In the folly of fun, we find the tryst.

Each chuckle contains a lesson so sweet,
With winks of insight, life feels complete.
So dance through the jest, and embrace the cheer,
For joy is the path when the end's not near.

Let laughter be the thread of our days,
With wisecracks and jests lighting our ways.
In this tapestry woven with wit and cheer,
Winks of wisdom guide us here.

Hilarity and Heart

With a quip and a giggle, we start the day,
Inviting the world to join in the play.
A dash of humor, a sprinkle of grace,
In laughter's embrace, we find our place.

The heart skips a beat with each silly pun,
Uniting us all, we're gleeful and fun.
Let's juggle our troubles, throw them in the air,
For laughter's a treasure, precious and rare.

In the circus of life, let's be the clowns,
With slapstick charm, we'll lighten the frowns.
So toss out the gloom, let joy take the lead,
In hilarity, love plants the seed.

With every chuckle, the heart finds its song,
In the rhythm of laughter, we all belong.
So share your joy, let it spread like art,
For the best kind of magic is humor with heart.

Witty Wanderings

In a world where socks go missing,
Laughter is the key, I'm wishing.
Take a walk, enjoy the jest,
Life's a game; give it your best.

Stumbling on a garden gnome,
He waved and said, "I'm not alone!"
With every step we trip and fall,
Yet giggles serve to break it all.

Frogs with crowns in a nearby stream,
Ribbiting dreams, or so it seems.
Hop along, don't take a pause,
For a laugh gives life a worthy cause.

A dancing cat with a silly hat,
Jiving to the beat, how about that?
Life's a circus, a joyful show,
With each deep chuckle, we surely grow.

Echoes of Encouragement

When clouds above seem gray and drear,
A smile can wipe away that fear.
A bubble pops in the air we chase,
Tickling hearts, it's a funny place.

An ant in shades struts his stuff,
"Life's a picnic, can't be too tough!"
While juggling crumbs, he winks with glee,
Finding joy in the smallest spree.

A rubber chicken stops for tea,
"Why so serious?" it asks with glee.
Great lessons wrapped in buoyant laughs,
Life's a puzzle; find the halves.

Puns like confetti fill the air,
Sprinkling joy everywhere.
Echoing laughter as we cheer,
In every quirk, we find our cheer.

The Humor in Hurdles

Life's hurdles come, tall and wide,
Yet laughter's there, right by your side.
Jumping high, or maybe not,
Make it playful, give it a shot.

A blender's mishap, smoothie surprise,
Fruits going flying, what a disguise!
Spilling joy, not just the drink,
In every mess, we'll find a wink.

A snail on a skateboard, moving slow,
With every bump, he steals the show.
Life's a track with ups and downs,
Wear your best smile, lose those frowns.

So leap and giggle with all your might,
Dance through troubles, it feels so right.
Through every fall, let laughter be,
The spark that sets your spirit free.

Journey of Wit and Whimsy

Maps may twist, and roads may bend,
But giggles will always be your friend.
A journey taken with a wink,
Turns the mundane into a link.

A parrot recites jokes on the fly,
"Polly wants humor," oh my, oh my!
Each feathered punchline fills the air,
Life's a treasure; laughter's rare.

A rollercoaster of puns and fun,
Screams and laughter, two-for-one.
Round every turn, quips take flight,
With cheeky grins, we win the night.

So grab a hat, wear it askew,
Twirl through life; it's all up to you.
In every step, find whimsy's kiss,
For a life well-lived, you can't miss!

The Jest for the Journey

Life's a puzzle, grab a piece,
In laughter's realm, we find our lease.
With every jest, a path unfolds,
The stories shared, worth more than gold.

Chasing dreams with silly grace,
A banana peel, a funny face.
In mishaps, we find our song,
Embrace the wrong; you can't go wrong.

Life's a circus, don't forget the show,
Every slide and slip helps us grow.
A joke or pun to light the way,
Turns a frown into a bright bouquet.

So giggle, cackle, laugh aloud,
In whimsy's arms, we stand so proud.
For every jest a lesson hides,
In the joyful ride, the heart abides.

Finding Your Funny

In the mirror, make a face,
Who knew humor had such grace?
With every laugh, we climb the wall,
Where joy resides, we never fall.

Kites of giggles float so high,
A silly thought can make you fly.
From awkward chats to joyful roars,
Every moment opens doors.

Chase the punchlines; don't just walk,
In every stumble, learn to talk.
Like a rubber chicken in a chair,
Life's absurd; embrace the dare.

So seek the chuckles, don't hold back,
In the world of wit, stay on track.
With laughter's torch, your path is bright,
Finding funny fills life's light.

Pantomimes of Purpose

Life's a show, the stage is set,
Dancing shoes, no need to fret.
With every slip, we find our stride,
In jest and giggles, we take pride.

The mime of dreams, a silent cheer,
Whisking away our doubt and fear.
A wink, a nod, a playful tease,
In laughter's grip, it's sure to please.

Each cue, each line, a chance to play,
In comedy's embrace, we sway.
With every act, a twist untold,
Life's jesters create memories bold.

So take your bow, the laughter's real,
In the pantomime, we freely feel.
Every giggle shapes the role,
In this grand play, we find our soul.

Wit and Whimsy intertwined

A wink at fate, a witty jest,
In life's great game, we do our best.
With every quip, we thread the line,
In whimsy's weave, our hearts align.

Painting smiles with humor's brush,
In playful moments, we feel the rush.
A pun here and there, brighten the day,
Where laughter lingers, we long to stay.

So dance with words, let spirits soar,
In comedy's embrace, we find our core.
Through chuckles and jests, the world's our stage,
Life's grand tale written page by page.

So lift your glass, toast to the fun,
Let's laugh together 'til the day is done.
With wit and whimsy hand in hand,
We create a joy that's simply grand.

Witty Compass: Navigating Life's Map

A map of dreams, oh what a sight,
With arrows pointing left and right.
Each twist and turn, a lively jest,
To find the path that suits us best.

When laughter leads the way you roam,
The journey feels just like your home.
With every chuckle, step you take,
You'll find the joy in every break.

In shadows cast by doubt and fear,
A giggle clears the fog, my dear.
For every blunder, watch and see,
A lesson wrapped in comedy.

So grab your compass, smile wide,
Together we'll enjoy the ride.
In maps of life, so bright and true,
The funny makes the world anew.

Laughing Our Way to Insight

With humor as our clever guide,
We roam the streets, we never hide.
Each giggle sparks a brilliant thought,
In every joke, new lessons caught.

The world's a stage, we dance around,
In silly shoes, together found.
For laughter's worth a thousand words,
In quiet whispers, truth occurs.

When troubles come to knock us down,
We swat them back with playful frown.
For every 'oops', a hearty cheer,
We'll laugh it off, our path is clear.

So let's embrace each goofy plot,
With every twist, we'll learn a lot.
In joy we find our guiding light,
As laughter shines through darkest night.

Grins Granted: A Guide to Existence

In life's grand book, let's turn the page,
With grins that sparkle, hearts engage.
A wink, a nod, a silly phrase,
Will light the path through foggy days.

Look for the puns that make you smile,
They're hidden gems, a funny style.
In every moment, joy will spark,
A firefly's dance in the dark.

When plans go wrong, don't fret, don't pout,
Just share a laugh, there's no doubt.
For in the mischief that we find,
The sweetest wisdom flows entwined.

So treasure laughter, keep it near,
It guides you well through path unclear.
With every smile and playful tease,
You'll find your way with perfect ease.

Quirks of Meaning in Every Moment

In quirks and giggles, life's a scene,
With snappy comebacks, bright and keen.
Each oddity, a clue in hand,
With silly steps, together we stand.

A pun here, a wink there,
In playful banter, love and care.
For every twist of fate we meet,
A chuckle turns it bittersweet.

Those silly moments, how they shine,
Turning mundane into divine.
With laughter bouncing off the walls,
We find real magic in the smalls.

So dance through life with joy enhanced,
Let every quirk give you a chance.
In all the humor that you find,
A joyful heart is always kind.

The Journey of Joyful Whimsy

Life's a dance, don't miss a beat,
Twist and twirl, no need for heat.
Chuckle loud, let laughter spread,
Joy's the map, just follow ahead.

Hop on clouds, float with the breeze,
Wear silly hats, indulge with ease.
Giggles echo through every lane,
Smile wide, let's make some gain.

With every step, a jump, a leap,
Catch the fun, dive in deep.
Wobble and wobble, sway to the sound,
In this whimsy, bliss is found.

Sassy Steps Forward

Strut with sass, don't hold it back,
Skip through life, find your own track.
Witty remarks in your back pocket,
Turn dull moments into a rocket.

Saunter boldly, heels in the air,
Tickle your toes, spin without care.
A wink and a nod as the day rolls by,
Make a scene, reach for the sky.

Jump in puddles, make a splash,
Dance with shadows, joy's a dash.
Life's a script, improvise well,
In every stumble, let laughter swell.

Slapstick Signposts

Trip on fate, tie your shoe tight,
Laugh at the falls, embrace the slight.
Signs say 'detour', but why not glide?
Slapstick humor is our guide.

Twist this way, then swing that,
Life's a circus, wear the hat.
With pies in the face, we'll find our way,
Laughter's the currency, come what may.

Bumps and giggles mark the path,
Take a moment, embrace the wrath.
Chase the sun, even in the rain,
Silly antics keep joy sustained.

The Pathway of Play

Through fields of laughter, we must roam,
Building our castles, finding our home.
Each step a game, with friends we cheer,
Playtime is endless, no need for fear.

Chasing shadows, tickling time,
Every minute sparkles, every second a rhyme.
Dive into puddles, splash with glee,
In this playful world, we're all so free.

Let's spin around until we're dizzy,
Laugh at ourselves, it's always busy.
With glimmers of fun lighting the way,
Join the journey, come out and play.

Laughs to Light the Way

In the dark, a chuckle bright,
A joke can turn the wrong to right.
With every stumble, a grin to show,
Laughter helps our worries go.

A wink is worth a thousand words,
Like flying high, or free as birds.
So let your punchlines find their mark,
And fill your journey with a spark.

When life serves lemons, add a twist,
A funny face, you can't resist.
Turn the sour into sweet delight,
And watch your spirits take to flight.

So stroll along this playful path,
With silly quips, embrace the laugh.
Each step you take, let joy unfurl,
For laughter is the best of pearls.

Heartfelt Humor

With loved ones near, the jokes take flight,
A shared giggle warms the night.
From puns that land like feathered cheer,
To tickles wrapped in bonds so dear.

A heart can thump from laughter's sway,
In every joke, a love relay.
The best of memories often blend,
With punchlines that around us send.

Life's little blunders, let's parley,
And turn them into comedy play.
For every tear that might have flowed,
There's humor waiting to unload.

So as we walk this winding road,
We'll carry laughs, a lightened load.
Through every twist the fate may lay,
Remember joy can lead the way.

A Giggle in Every Step

With every step, a chuckle springs,
Each moment caused by playful things.
A trip, a slip—don't take offense,
Just laugh along and build suspense.

A wink exchanged, a pun well-timed,
Find joy in every day we climb.
For life's a game, a jolly ride,
With humor as our joyful guide.

So if you stumble, laugh it off,
Make merry with the silly scoff.
For all the challenges we meet,
There's laughter waiting at our feet.

Embrace the light as we all tread,
With giggles soft, and smiles widespread.
Let happiness and humor blend,
And find the fun that has no end.

Playful Plots and Plans

Today's the day we set our schemes,
With jest and jive, we chase our dreams.
Each plot a twist, each plan a hoot,
A dash of mischief, oh so cute.

In every meeting, drop a line,
Where laughter flows, the hearts align.
For every goal can twist and bend,
When humor turns our foes to friends.

So scribble down those dreams with flair,
Add jokes and puns, show that you care.
Let's map this course with joyous zest,
And let our laughter be the best.

As scenes unfold, and tales are spun,
We'll gather giggles, have some fun.
For life is bright when we conspire,
To weave our days with laughter's fire.

The Path of Playful Serenity

In the garden of giggles, we dance so bright,
With laughter as our compass, we soar like flight.
Chasing clouds of whimsy, we glide and sway,
Finding joy in missteps, come what may.

Unicorns in sneakers, they skip with flair,
Ticklish rainbows giggle, light as air.
Every stumble a tickle, a playful tease,
Life's a funny riddle that aims to please.

So let's frolic through moments, with zest and cheer,
Snatching smiles like candies, in a world so dear.
When the road seems rocky, just take a ride,
On the bouncy castle where dreams abide.

Jokes that Guide Us Home

Why did the chicken cross over the street?
To discover the punchline, oh what a feat!
With a wink and a smirk, it took a chance,
Finding wisdom in giggles, a quirky dance.

Maps of giggles lead us to strange doors,
Where slapstick moments become our chores.
Navigating with humor, we laugh and roam,
Every quip a step closer to our home.

In life's funny theater, we play our part,
Treasuring each chuckle, a work of art.
With laughter as our lantern, we'll never stray,
In this jest of a journey, it's all okay!

Life's Silly Signposts

Signs that point to laughter, they line the way,
"Caution! Slapstick Ahead!" they gleefully say.
The detours of joy, they twist and turn,
In the book of life, it's laughter we learn.

Bumpy roads of giggles, they make us sway,
While rubber chickens lead us astray.
Every detour a chance for a silly reprieve,
In the playground of life, we truly believe.

With a wink from the sky and a pun from the ground,
We rock with the laughter, in joy we're found.
So let's frolic in folly, let our hearts chime,
In this carnival ride, let's gibber and rhyme!

Dramedy of Decisions

In the theater of choices, the spotlight shines,
Should we wear silly hats or dance in lines?
With every decision, a quirky twist,
In the play of our lives, nothing's amiss.

Should I pick the green beans or the gumball tree?
Every choice is a hoot, pure comedy!
With a laugh track rolling, the plot thickens fast,
Dancing through decisions, let the fun last.

So we juggle our fates, like clowns on a stage,
With every mishap, we turn the page.
The drama may linger, but with laughter we cope,
For life's a grand dramedy, filled with hope.

The Quest for Meaningful Merriment

In the quest for joy, we set our sail,
Chasing giggles that never pale.
Life's a jest, a playful spree,
Finding laughs is the key, you see.

With each quirk and each pun,
We dance beneath the sun.
A wink, a nudge, a subtle tease,
Joyful hearts are sure to please.

In the pursuit of simple bliss,
We stumble into humorous miss.
Twists of fate and comic tales,
Laughter always prevails.

So gather round, let spirits soar,
Crack a joke, then ask for more.
Life's a comedy, absurdly bright,
In laughter's warm and glowing light.

Serve Up Some Significance

Serve up life with a twist of fun,
A scoop of humor, everyone!
Whisk the frowns with a hearty cheer,
Mix in laughter as the main career.

Cook the day with jokes on the side,
Let silliness be the cherished guide.
A dash of wit in every bite,
Stirring smiles from morning to night.

Plates of purpose piled high,
Banquets fit for giggles nearby.
Life's buffet, where joy's the main dish,
Dig in deep, it's the only wish.

So serve it warm, don't skimp on the fun,
Life's best when laughter's spun.
Through the chaos, food for the heart,
With every pun, we play our part.

Laughter's Lantern: Lighting the Way

With laughter's light, we find our path,
Banish the clouds, escape the wrath.
Chuckle bright like a glowing star,
Illuminating just who we are.

In every giggle, a beacon's glow,
Puns and jests, our hearts shall grow.
Witty banter as fuel for the ride,
Guided by joy, we won't subside.

The winding roads may twist and bend,
But laughter, dear friend, is a godsend.
With each punchline, our spirits soar,
Embrace the fun, forevermore.

Let's raise our lanterns, shine them bright,
In the dark, let humor ignite.
For in this life's intricate dance,
A laugh can spark a second chance.

Jokes on the Journey

On life's grand journey, laughs abound,
With puns and quips, the joy is found.
Travel light with a funny bone,
Every mile marks a punchline grown.

From detours filled with silly sights,
To chances for ridiculous delights.
When hurdles come, don't lose your spark,
With laughter loud, it lights the dark.

So roll with the punches, take a chance,
Life's a jesting, merry dance.
Leave worries aside and hear the cheer,
Jokes are the compass that keeps us near.

As we wander through life's twists and turns,
Let humor be the fire that burns.
For jokes on this journey, what a find,
The best of times, just intertwined.

Lighthearted Life Lessons

When you chase a dream, don't wear tight shoes,
You'll stumble and trip, and be left with the blues.
A laughter-filled space is the best kind of tool,
Remember to smile, it's the utmost rule.

If life gives you lemons, make a fun pie,
Throw in some giggles, and give it a try.
Plant seeds of good humor, watch flowers they grow,
A garden of laughter, oh what a show!

If you're feeling down, put on a great hat,
Get silly and dance, with your favorite cat.
Life's not just serious, it's a grand canter,
With each twist and turn, there's room for romance here.

So keep your chin up, and don't take the bait,
Jokes turned to wisdom can never be late.
Sprinkle your days with a fine sense of quirk,
And live with a chuckle, just watch how it works!

Chasing Cheer

In a world that is serious, find joy in the jest,
A quip in the corner can brighten a fest.
Run wild with your grins, let laughter abound,
In the race for delight, let happiness be found.

A pun here and there is a treasure to keep,
Toss them like confetti; let giggles leap.
Wear socks that don't match, and dance like a fool,
Embrace all the quirks; they're the best life's tool!

Chase sunshine like kites, on a breezy day,
Let worries all scatter, blow them away.
Smile at the clouds, and give them a wink,
With laughter as glue, our hearts will not sink.

So gather your friends, and share a good laugh,
Life's grand rollercoaster is better by half.
A joke and a smile can heal even the ache,
So sprinkle good humor, it's never too late!

Anecdotes of Aspiration

In pursuit of your dreams, don't trip on a shoe,
For sneaky old shoes love to play peek-a-boo.
Step lively each morning, with mischief in mind,
For life's little quirks hide treasures to find.

Tell tales of your fumbles, wear them with pride,
Like badges of honor, let them be your guide.
Turning stumbles to stories, like cakes from the pan,
Laughter's the spice of an ambitious plan.

If plans go awry, just laugh at the blunder,
A spark of confusion might lead to some thunder.
With each wild misstep, there's a lesson in glee,
Find joy in the journey so silly and free!

So pen down the moments, the giggles, the stings,
For life's greatest tales come with flaps and with flings.
In this tale of existence, find fun in the plot,
With humor as armor, you'll worry a lot!

Satirical Shadows

In the theater of life, slip on a big shoe,
Comedy thrives where the oddities brew.
Let's jest with our shadows, find humor in light,
For seriousness fades with a tickling bite.

Wit's like an umbrella when storms start to roam,
It keeps you all dry when you won't stay at home.
Laugh at the chaos, dance in the street,
Every chuckle a rhythm, every giggle a beat.

Beware of the frowns that lurk round each bend,
For laughter's a balm, it's the perfect blend.
Share puns with the moon, let your worries take flight,
In shadows of giggles, all darkness feels bright.

So grab every chuckle, hold it real tight,
For life's but a jest, amidst day and night.
In satire's sweet sway, we find all our grace,
So dance with your shadows, and brighten this place!

Finding Meaning in Mirth

In the garden of chuckles, we play,
Each giggle a flower, come what may.
Life's silly riddles keep us light,
Dancing through shadows, oh what a sight!

With each little blunder, we find our way,
Tripping on humor, we seize the day.
Seriousness fades like a dress shirt on fire,
Laughter's the fuel, and joy's our attire!

Each knock on the head's a lesson to heed,
Building up laughter from every misdeed.
When fortune's a jester, the world's a stage,
Gather 'round friends, let's turn the page!

For life's just a joke if you stop to laugh,
A comic strip dreaming, our silly path.
Find meaning in giggles, let smiles unfurl,
Each laugh a treasure, come join the whirl!

The Jest of Existence

Life's a punchline, never quite clear,
A tickle that traces both far and near.
In slapstick moments we find our role,
Cartwheels of chaos, we stroll with our soul.

When reason gets lost in a tumble and roll,
We laugh off the stumbles, a vibrant goal.
A wink and a nudge, we share the delight,
Finding our fortune in the bright moonlight.

In the circus of living, we juggle our fears,
Each joke a balloon that deflates with our tears.
So join in the fun, take the stage and play,
For laughter's the compass that shows us the way!

With each comedic twist and absurd plot,
The jest of existence connects us a lot.
So gather the giggles, keep them in sight,
And toast to the laughter that makes us feel right!

Whimsical Whys

Why does the chicken cross roads in a whip?
Just to find out if life's a funny trip?
With questions that boggle and riddles that tease,
We chase after giggles, like children at ease.

The world's full of quirks, like socks with no pairs,
Lessons in laughter are found everywhere.
So let's ask the whys, with a chuckle to spare,
What's life without whimsy, in sunshine and air?

In the garden of jest, where serendipity blooms,
We paint with our laughter, dispelling the glooms.
For every wisecrack is a step on our quest,
To find the right punchline, which truly feels best.

Why dwell on the heavy? Let's lighten the load,
With giggles and gags along this strange road.
So tip your hat to the funny and spry,
For the whimsical whys make our spirits fly!

Laughter's Life Compass

With laughter as a compass, we navigate wide,
Finding joy in the detours, where silly resides.
A chuckle can shift our whole point of view,
And turn every mishap into something new.

In the map of adventures, with funny as true,
Each smile a landmark, let's gather a slew.
From puns and pratfalls, we learn and we grow,
Life's a ride of hilarity, come join the show!

The jokes that we tell as the moments unfold,
Are treasures more precious than diamonds or gold.
So steer with your laughter, let giggles ignite,
For laughter's the beacon, our continuous flight!

So chart your course boldly, where smiles intertwine,
A voyage of humor is simply divine.
For in every soft chuckle, a lesson we find,
Laughter's life compass, forever aligned!

Laugh Lines and Life's Designs

In life's great sketch, we draw and doodle,
With winks and chuckles, we cut through the poodle.
Each giggle a stroke, on canvas so bright,
Artfully crafted, in laughter, we write.

We dance on the edge of a playful mistake,
Like bakers, we rise when we crack up a cake.
With each belly laugh, a wrinkle appears,
Smiles fill the gaps, dispelling our fears.

A pun is a bridge that connects with a grin,
It's laughter that makes stubborn hearts spin.
So gather your friends, share jokes on the fly,
In this quirky circus, the sillies can fly.

So live like a clown in a world full of fright,
With a tickle, a joke, and a dash of delight.
For life is a party, let's dance in the rain,
With laughter as fuel, we'll forget our refrain.

Playful Pearls of Wisdom

A wise man once said, 'Don't take it too hard,'
Life's treasure is laughter, and we're the reward.
In moments of folly, true wisdom may nest,
Like geese on a pond, let joy be your quest.

When life gives you lemons, make lemonade fun,
In the grand game of life, let your spirit run.
Toss puns like confetti, let happiness bloom,
In the grand scheme, your laughter's the room.

Chase dreams like a kid, with a kite in the sky,
Finding light in the shadows, give each chance a try.
In the carnival world, we all play our part,
With jokes as our tickets and giggles to start.

So gather your pearls, from the ocean of jest,
In the sea of existence, just give it your best.
In laughter and mischief, we flourish and thrive,
Join the parade of the joyful, alive!

A Symphony of Smiles and Seeking

Hear the laughter, a vibrant refrain,
A symphony plays, with joy as our gain.
In each quirky note, we find our sweet song,
Through ups and through downs, it's where we belong.

Chasing the sunshine, we frolic and play,
With each laugh shared, we lighten the day.
The melody swells, as our spirits take flight,
In this whimsical dance, the world feels just right.

For truth wears a smile, so wear it with pride,
Explore every corner, let giggles be our guide.
In the concert of life, let laughter be clear,
Every chuckle a note, a moment to cheer.

So let us be seekers, of fun and delight,
A riddle, a pun, shining ever so bright.
Together we'll laugh through the highs and the lows,
In this symphony of smiles, our friendship just grows.

The Balance of Banter and Being

In the dance of existence, we twirl and we spin,
With banter like bubbles, we float with a grin.
Each quip a reminder, that life can be light,
So let's juggle our joy, till the stars are in sight.

A wink and a nod, we balance our cheer,
Like tightrope walkers, there's nothing to fear.
Each joke is a hug that we freely bestow,
In moments of laughter, our true selves we show.

So throw in a pun, make the world take a pause,
With light-hearted banter, we soften our flaws.
While seriousness lurks, at the fringe of each jest,
In the garden of laughter, we find our sweet rest.

For life is a circus, let's enjoy the parade,
With smiles as our tickets, we'll never evade.
In this jolly ballet, we sway to the beat,
Finding harmony sweet, where the funny can meet.

The Laughing Lantern

In the night a lantern glows,
With jokes it brightly shows.
A giggle here, a chuckle there,
Laughter dances in the air.

Life's twists come with comic flair,
With every twist, a grin we wear.
An ill-timed joke makes spirits soar,
Just when you think you've heard it all before.

A punchline hidden in the breeze,
Finds you laughing 'neath the trees.
Though paths seem dark and stormy too,
A giggle can light up the view.

So carry jokes, let laughter lead,
In every heart, plant a humorous seed.
For life's absurdity, make it fun,
And watch as all your blues are undone.

Wit's Wayfarer's Journey

A traveler with wit so bright,
Chases sun with pure delight.
Every stop requires a jest,
A quick quip that's truly zest.

On winding roads, the laughter flows,
With every turn, a new joke grows.
A pun, a play, oh what a scene,
Each moment thrives; it bursts, it beams.

At borders where the funny hides,
A clever pun, the heart abides.
With every chuckle, maps unfold,
A journey vast, a story told.

So pack your laughs, they're worth the trip,
Life's too short for a solemn flip.
With a wink and a bright winkled eye,
Dance through life, let humor fly.

Smiles that Steer

A smile's a compass, that's for sure,
It points to joys that we all adore.
With laughter as our guiding star,
We navigate where wonders are.

Through twists and turns, with jokes we go,
A punchline here, a chuckle low.
In every frown, a wink may hide,
Unlock the fun and let it glide.

In our sails, our laughter steers,
Filling the sails, calming our fears.
For life's a ship upon a sea,
With smiles that guide, we're truly free.

So gather round, let jests ignite,
In quirks and quirks, find endless delight.
Adventures await with laughter near,
Let giggles and grins be your steer.

The Breezy Bulletin of Being

A bulletin floats on a breeze,
Filled with jests that aim to please.
It whispers jokes from tree to tree,
Each pun a present, wild and free.

Readers chuckle, giggle wide,
As laughter rolls like an ocean tide.
Every line a ticklish tease,
Bringing warmth like sunny ease.

With headlines bold, and puns galore,
This bulletin never feels a bore.
Each page turned, more smiles arise,
As laughter lifts us to the skies.

So share this joy, let it not cease,
In every life, find your own piece.
For humor's charm, life's sweetest thing,
Is like a breeze that makes hearts sing.

www.ingramcontent.com/pod-product-compliance
Lightning Source LLC
Chambersburg PA
CBHW051700160426
43209CB00004B/966